We Are Climbers, All

A Book of
Positive and Uplifting Poems

with Poet's Literary Analysis
and Personal Comments

Tom Blaisse

We Are Climbers, All

Copyright © 2012 Tom Blaisse. All rights reserved.

No part of this book may be used or reproduced in any form or by any electronic or mechanical means including information storage and retrieval systems, without written permission from the author. The only exception is by a reviewer, who may quote short excerpts (but not any complete poem) in a review.

All images are from public domain or used with permission.

Book Interior Design, Copyediting, and Typography: Biz Burnett
Book Cover Design: Michelle Blais (www.DenimDesignDiva.com)

Printed in the United States of America

ISBN-10:   1480165239
ISBN-13: 978-1480165236

DEDICATION

To My Family:

My wife Cookie,
My children Matthew, Michael, and Beth,

All of whom have given me the motivation
to continue to climb my mountain.

ACKNOWLEDGMENTS

I would like to thank...

...my wife, Cookie, for her inspiration and support. I love you more than words can convey for sharing this mountain-climbing adventure so faithfully every step of the way.

...my sister, Biz Burnett, for her editing, design, and research services and support during this publishing and marketing process. I appreciate very much her literary expertise and coaching.

...those who provided reviews: Joe Chelius, Diana Weiss, Tom Lipinski, and Rory Aplanalp. Thank you for understanding and offering your insights about my mission and how this book can benefit my readers.

...all the people in my life over the years who were part of the experiences that inspired these poems. Thank you for helping me remember we are all each other's Teachers <u>and</u> Students.

INTRODUCTION

Tom Blaisse, *Poet/Author*

I am a teacher by trade. My mission is to help people learn and grow. You'll see on my website (www.TomBlaisse.com) that my "byline" is "Turning on lights so people can shine."

I taught High School English, Speech, and Drama for 7 years after college. During that time, I completed my Master's Degree in Counseling Psychology. Then I realized I really didn't want to be a School Guidance Counselor. So I "jumped ship," not knowing on what shore I would land.

I found my niche in Adult Education and Corporate Training, by serving a type of post-graduate apprenticeship with a small consulting firm in the Philadelphia area. My mentor taught me a lot about working with corporate Training & Development clients, how to customize Leadership and Communication Skills programs, and how to facilitate workshops. After a brief stint as in-house Director of Training & Development for Hershey Entertainment and Resort Co., I landed my "dream job" as a Seminar Leader for (the then) Franklin Quest Co., which later merged with the Covey Leadership Center, to become FranklinCovey Co. Over a period of almost 11 years, I conducted more than 1,800 live seminars, mostly on the topic of *Time Management*. When that "chapter" of my career ended in 2000, and after a few brief stints elsewhere, I decided to go out on my own as an independent Speaker, Trainer, and Management Consultant.

Along the way, I assembled these poems that I had written over a period of many years. I edited them, and added some new ones. This book is the result of that effort. Some poems are easy to understand on the surface; others might need some further explanation. They all follow the theme of "climbing our (proverbial) mountain," with the three chapters—"On Learning," "On Loving," and "On Living"—focusing on those specific sub-themes. In the "Commentaries" section, I provide, for each poem, some literary analysis on the Structure, Imagery, and Themes, and also a Personal Comment. As with all poetry, interpretation is always open to the reader. I simply offer my thoughts to aid in the appreciation of the philosophy and perspective of each poem. I realize that the style, format, and messages of these poems are vastly different from those you may have read in high school or college. Perhaps they are a new genre of poetry.

May you continue to learn, love, and live joyfully as you climb your own mountain.

CONTENTS

CHAPTER ONE
On Learning

What Makes
  People Learn?.......3

Reality:
  Check It Out 4

Learning Through
  Love 6

Talent 7

The Challenge
  of Change............ 8

Dear God.............10

Evening Prayers ...11

To The Teacher ... 12

CHAPTER TWO
On Loving

My Dear Child 15

You Are Good 16

It Doesn't Work 17

All Relationships
  Serve a Purpose....18

Our Loved Ones.....19

We Are Family....... 20

At the Fireside 22

A Fair..................... 24

Garden Flower...... 25

My Deer, Do Not Lay
  Hurting — Part I ... 26

My Dear, Do Not Lay
  Hurting — Part II .. 27

Common Cents 29

CHAPTER THREE
On Living

The Miracles
  of Life 33

Little Kids............. 34

A Director's
  Note.................... 36

The Chess Game ... 37

Or What's a
  Heaven For?......... 38

The Candle
  Flame..................40

The Productivity
  Pyramid 41

Just Do It! 42

Renewal................ 43

We Are Climbers,
  All........................44

Commentaries 47

About the
  Author 79

CHAPTER ONE
On Learning

WHAT MAKES PEOPLE LEARN?

What makes people learn?
HATRED,
    PAIN,
        CONFLICT,
            REVENGE,
                ANGER,
                    LONELINESS,
                        DEATH.

What makes people learn?
STABILITY,
    RELIEF,
        RESOLUTION,
            FORGIVENESS,
                PEACE,
                    FRIENDSHIP,
                      LOVE.

What makes people learn?
ACCEPTANCE,
    CONFIDENCE,
        HEALTH,
            FAITH,
                COURAGE,
                    GENEROSITY,
                      LIFE.

A condition opens up one's eyes
To a separate reality of choice.
It punctuates the difference between
What is and what could be.
It motivates to change.

What makes people learn?
FREEDOM.

Tom Blaisse

REALITY: CHECK IT OUT
(written from the perspective of a
"troubled teen" being challenged to change)

I see my friends at this school assembly,
Lost in space, pierced with anger,
Headphones pounding, blocking feeling.
Hey, why am I here anyway?

I'm holding back while crying out.
My force field's up; let no one in.
Draw and doodle all the day,
Until it's time for the next escape.

I've given up, long ago.
Why pretend there's something more?
Does anybody really care?
The teachers, maybe; but I don't get it.

You say, "Beliefs lead to behavior,
The results of which should meet my needs."
Hey, sex and drugs and rock 'n roll
Are all I need; they get results.

Reality? You check it out.
I'm O.K. Are you O.K.?
It's not my problem; blame someone else:
Parents, schools, the cops, the courts.

I'm tired of playing by their rules.
Why am I here anyway?
Is it time to leave? I gotta go.
I'm done with this Reality Check.

We Are Climbers, All

I would rather play and party;
Work some, maybe, to buy my fun.
"Red light flashing? Must pull over;
Band-aids are a short-term fix."

That kinda makes some sense, I guess.
"Nothing will change until I change it."
"I have control of my own life."
Why am I here anyway?

Escape behaviors will get me nowhere.
Reality comes creeping back.
Perhaps I'd better check it out,
And challenge now myself to change.

If my self-worth is based on others,
I will never meet my needs.
Some pleasure, maybe; temporary.
But not results I may really want.

I'll set some goals, then break them down.
Commit the time to work my plan.
Chip away at that huge boulder,
And over time, I'll see results.

I'll let go of my hostility,
And stop all this insanity.
I'll check out who I want to be,
And create my own Reality.

Tom Blaisse

LEARNING THROUGH LOVE

Why must we Learn through Sin?
    We slip and slide through fields of dung,
    And force the dirt upon our brows.
    We laugh at our iniquities,
    Then cry to see our deeds foreclosed.

Why must we Learn through Pain?
    We step upon our stony faults,
    And kneel down with broken backs.
    We harbor anger and malcontent,
    Then fall below the suffering sands.

Why must we Learn through Fear?
    We creep in shallow water holes,
    And hide from Truth that stands erect.
    We fly and fall, feeling no faith,
    Then sink into a shattered haven.

Why can't we Learn through Love?
    We'd lift our souls above the Earth,
    And let our God disciple us.
    We'd foster Courage in a calming state,
    Then breeze unfurled in Love's embrace.

We Are Climbers, All

TALENT

Talent is, to us, God's Gift:
  A Refinement of the Mind.
  Buried if not explored.
  Must be coupled with desire.

Talent is our second Nature:
  Where it lives, Energy abides.
  It cannot go unchallenged.
  It will be found by those who search.

Talent is for us a Bell:
  Silent until the Chime is rung.
  A Call unanswered for a while,
  Until the Sound can't be ignored.

Talent is the Mustard Seed:
  From just a little, will spring a lot.
  It moves mountains from faith to action,
  So Barrenness becomes Fertility.

Talent lies within us all:
  Believe it not and lose Life's Purpose.
  To Work, to Play, to Think in any Form,
  Creative Expression is an Attitude toward the World.

Talent: Use It or Be Sad.

Tom Blaisse

The Challenge of Change

Can someone truly change,
And move oneself from then to now,
And break a mold so surely set?

Can someone truly change,
And rise above a useless thought,
And forge a new belief?

Can someone truly change,
And reconstruct an angry list,
And make it more productive stress?

I say Yes!
When the need is great,
Purpose is solid in the heart.

I say Yes!
When sights are raised,
The soul is moved to start.

I say Yes!
When resolve is sure,
Intention is pure.

We Are Climbers, All

For wisdom grows when it is nurtured,
And fruits of patience seen.
Then virtue plows a road less taken,
Which leads to Inner Peace.

Follow then your path to change,
And do not fear the shift,
Nor miss the old unseemly ways,
Which leave you flat and weak.

The butterfly does not lament
The loss of its cocoon.
But it rejoices when Time calls
To shed its onetime haven.

Then love what you have lived to learn,
And strive to live that Truth.
So conscience can be ever free,
And health forever thine.

Tom Blaisse

Dear God

Will my heart be spared?
Oh, let me know it!
   Will I weather the tempest that has been set upon me?
   Will I feel Your peace inject me with acceptance?
   Will I be hurled into the light of Your Love?

Let me embrace Your warmth and understanding!
Let me know that You are with me, that I am not alone;
   That in the Darkness, there is Light;
   That in the Abyss, there is Foundation;
   That in the Loss, there is Hope.

My trust is waning; I know not where to turn!
I cannot see when my eyes are closed.
   Enlighten me to see through Your eyes.
   Energize me to hear through Your ears.
   Empower me to feel through Your strength.

My love cries out from its will to grow in a world of weeds!
The Passion I bear is both a burden and a joy.
   To whom shall I deliver?

Dear God, hold me here, while my thoughts call up!
And in the hour of my recognition,
   Let me touch the Truth of Your Word ;
   Let me taste the Bread of Your Life ;
   Let me drink the Wine of Your Salvation ;
Until the day when Joy is finally found,
And I bask in the Summer of my contentment.

We Are Climbers, All

EVENING PRAYERS

So long ago,
    When I was new and fresh
    And thus attached to God,
I would speak my message to Him,
While kneeling nightly at the household hamper.

With some suspicion from big sister
    Why I would choose that place
    To talk to God,
Each night in peace, He would be there,
Above the family clothes.

With privacy of thought,
    And such clairvoyance against that wall,
    Praying prettily and expecting much,
No knowledge of the curves that lay ahead,
A perfect dream was I then.

Since then, though drifted, sifted thoughts
    Collect as dew that dries past dawn,
    To return again unarmed except for faith,
I do foresee a child's life again.
No hamper now.

Lord, hear my call
    Whene'er I speak
    In softness or with sharper tongue.
It is the plea of Your own servant,
Once fed in innocence.

For knowing darkness, my thoughts surrender.
    To you I am betrothed,
    With strength, endurance, and courage offered.
I bow to hamper none.
Your will be done.

Tom Blaisse

TO THE TEACHER

In the midst of indecision
    When this world seems split apart,
And the joy of what was once safe
    Turns solid in the heart;

In these days of growing wonderment
    When confusion rears its head,
And time is twisted, tightly, slightly,
    To find so many dead;

In the work that lasts forever
    When answers can't be found,
And so many of us turn our heads
    With tearful, fearful frowns:

You surpass that gory doubt,
    And finger through the mire,
To lighten up so many minds,
    And cultivate desire.

CHAPTER TWO
On Loving

We Are Climbers, All

My Dear Child

I will haunt you
       For the good of you within.
I will mystify you
       Beyond your wildest imaginations.
I will greet you
       With nothing but smiles, ever.
I will pardon you
       Each time you truly wish it.

I will haunt you
       For the good of you within.
I will rescue you
       When you are drowning in despair.
I will cast out those demons
       Who taunt you with their anger.
I will love you, as a child
       Who has been lost and now is found.

I will haunt you
     For the good of you within.
I will nurture and enrich you
     When you are starving for My Love.
I will praise and admonish you
     For your deeds and your conceit.
I will grant you your desires
     When your faith equals your effort.

I will haunt you
       For the good of you within.
And you'll be welcomed home with me, in Paradise.

As Always,
God

Tom Blaisse

YOU ARE GOOD

You are Good,
>As an eye perceives the light,
>As a day receives the night,
>As a mind conceives what's right.

You are Good,
>As a dream consumes all thought,
>As a coach assumes what's taught,
>As a breeze resumes for naught.

You are Good,
>As a smile portrays what's told,
>As a book conveys what's old,
>As a hug delays the cold.

You are Good,
>As a heart respects a song,
>As a love detects what's wrong,
>As a soul protects what's strong.

You are Good.

We Are Climbers, All

IT DOESN'T WORK

To pass on a hurt just doesn't work.
    It's Pain, unceasing and ever growing.
    A shallow fortress, a baseless hold.
    It merely fronts a show of strength;
    Cannot protect, but only hides.
    It cannot serve to patch one's sores.

To pass on a hurt just doesn't work.
    For underneath, the dampness swells.
    The solid bars fall soft and bend;
    Slip, then sink, now deeper down,
    Until, the means no longer just,
    Returns diminish; the hurt springs back.

To pass on a hurt just doesn't work.
    For the other's pain, in swampy sadness,
    Pervades the muck and clogs one's scope.
    No beams leak out; no joy is born.
    With braces tight, no route is clear
    To escape the torment self-imposed.

To forgive a hurt is what does work.
    For the truth reveals the courage needed
    To rise above and loosen the bonds
    That bar the healing from seeping through.
    When clouds are lifted, and freedom reigns,
    It's joy unceasing and ever growing.

Tom Blaisse

ALL RELATIONSHIPS SERVE A PURPOSE

All relationships serve a purpose:
    A mix for making each other smart,
    A match for tearing each other apart.
They help us to grow.

All relationships serve a purpose:
    For they are here, each for a season;
    And we are here, each for a reason.
They help us to flow.

All relationships serve a purpose:
    To smooth out the edges; to pull out the hue.
    Living together, so one can be two.
They help us to glow.

All relationships serve a purpose:
    Sometimes we get grain; sometimes we get rain.
    Then we plow the fields all over again.
They help us to sow.

All relationships serve a purpose:
    Then, what to our wondering hearts should appear
    But a cup full of Love, sometimes spiked with a tear.
They help us to know.

All relationships serve a purpose:
    The road must be clear in order to love.
    When roadblocks are up, all we do is just shove.
They help us to go.

We Are Climbers, All

OUR LOVED ONES

We'll always love the ones we've loved;
    They'll warm our hearts forever.
Their names might be a prayer,
But we will be aware
    Of their presence in God's world.

We may no longer touch their hands
    Nor see their faces gleam,
Nor hear their voices sparkle in our lives.
But our love for them will stay
    Until our journey's end.

No wash can wipe away the spot;
    No years can change the memories
Of how we loved them once.
For in many ways, we love them still.
    God allows our spirits to touch.

We might prefer to deny this truth,
    And choose to harbor pain.
The icy chill can pierce the day
As snow-capped mountains laugh in victory.
    But the beauty of what was will win.

The God of Time will set us free.
    And when we stand at Heaven's Gate
And see each loved one who has passed,
We'll know the ones we've loved
    Will warm our souls forever.

Tom Blaisse

WE ARE FAMILY

We are Family:
    Brothers and Sisters are we,
    Sharing moments as they come;
    Laughing, living, crying some;
    Taking life at life's own pace;
    Working, eating, saying grace.
We are Family.

We are Family:
    Neighbors all are we,
    Walking, talking, swapping tools;
    Socializing at swimming pools;
    Sharing rides to get a rest;
    Helping others to be their best.
We are Family.

We are Family:
    Church members are we,
    Praying to our special Lord;
    Contributing what we can afford;
    Baking cakes, holding hands;
    Supporting missions in far-off lands.
We are Family.

We Are Climbers, All

We are Family:
    Company workers are we,
    Joining forces to reach a goal;
    Helping each other to pay life's toll;
    Problem solving, decision making;
    Sometimes giving, sometimes taking.
We are Family.

We are Family:
    Nations all are we,
    Giving food to those in need;
    Sowing foreign lands with seed;
    Tolerating others' dance;
    Stopping wars—giving peace a chance.
We are Family.

We are Family:
    Spirits in Heaven are we,
    Different clans and companies,
    Churches, neighbors, and countries;
    Yellow, red, black, and white,
    All the same in God's sight.
We are Family.

Tom Blaisse

AT THE FIRESIDE

A FIRE KINDLES FROM A SINGLE MATCH.
THE PAPER, CRUMPLED, LIES IN PLACE,
AND SPLINTERS OF WOOD ARE DRESSED IN STYLE
SO AIR MAY SMARTLY JOIN WITH FUEL.
THE NEED IS STRONG IN THE COLD, BLUE ROOM.

THE TIPS THEN LIGHTED ON VARIED SIDES
MAKE CORNERS COME AGLOW AT ONCE.
'TIL UP IN FLAME THE FIRE GHOST
HAUNTS THE SOUL ALIVE WITH WARMTH,
AND BRIGHTENS EYES AND SKIES ALIKE.

A CRACKLING BLITZ TURNS WOOD TO COALS
THAT SERVE TO CRADLE WHAT'S NEWLY BORN.
THE LOGS, WELL PLACED, STAND SHOUTING NOW,
AND BLARE A TRIUMPHANT TRUMPET CALL
THAT PIQUES A PURRING FROM WITHIN.

A TENDER BREEZE IS JUST ENOUGH
FOR FLAME TO STRETCH AND GATHER STRENGTH.
THE VIBRANT HEAT BEGINS TO SPEAK
OF HUNGER FROM ITS WILL TO GROW.
THE PASSION LEAPS FROM LOVE LONG LIVED.

SO UP AND DOWN THE FIRE FLARES,
EACH PIECE IT EATS, PUFFED UP WITH AIR,
AND WATCHFUL EYES GIVE NOURISHMENT
TO KEEP THIS HEALTHY FLAME IN SHAPE,
SO DROWSINESS DOES NOT DRIFT IN.

We Are Climbers, All

But some time later, when the fuel is gone,
And not a whistle can be made,
The steam subsides; the rainbow fades.
And prodded not to stay aflame,
The one-time warmth now turns to cold.

The fire dwindles to light upon
The glowing thoughts of what was there.
The fading stars are shunned by ash,
And clouds of smoke pollute the air,
And still the will to stay awake.

The hour, late, 'tis sleeping time.
All twinkles dim; the flue is closed,
And blankets serve as surrogates.
"Good night, sweet love, May the gift of life
Arise again upon the morn."

The next day's sun, a vague recall,
But then more vivid as desire shouts,
"Is nothing left inside this soot?
Will not one red poke through this gray?
Oh God, there's hope where love abides!"

With little wood but strength of breath,
A flame ignites, then cries for more,
And boasts for joy that it did not die.
New fire kindled from a single ember—
A truth we must each day remember.

Tom Blaisse

A FAIR

The carnie flair of grease and sweat;
The stepping stones scratching soles;
The smell of food inviting taste;
The glare of work's impounded days;
Incites the mood with sunny strokes.

The once-forgotten tire tread;
The doll that's waiting for the win;
The smiling Smurf so neatly dressed;
The wonder of which ball to throw;
Invites a life in altered form.

The breezy talk that freely flows;
The thrill of ride's impending glee;
The sound of winning not yet felt;
The tempting touch so timely matched;
Ignites a tacit, placid glow.

We Are Climbers, All

GARDEN FLOWER

I see this flower in my garden,
    Has weathered the currents of the Fall,
And may survive unless downtrodden.
    Must I care for it at all?

Should it be pruned and fertilized,
    To give it strength to not be lost?
Or must it stand alone, untouched,
    So it can melt into the frost?

Perhaps I'll take it in to warm;
    With nurtured softness, help it grow.
Or would it wither out of place?
    No. Let it stand for the wind to blow.

For a flower grows best when undisturbed
    And left to find its own rebirth.
Then I'll reach out, to share its life.
    I love my flower for all its worth.

Tom Blaisse

MY DEER, DO NOT LAY HURTING — PART I

Tonight, I think a deer was hurt,
As it jumped from its abode.
I saw it run down through the woods,
And leap across the road.

I heard the squeal of the braking car.
I prayed that it would swerve.
The driver must have been surprised
To spot it at the curve.

I wish that deer had looked both ways,
To see if cars were coming.
She seemed to be in such a hurry
As I stepped out back while humming.

And without looking either way,
I walked into the night.
I did not stop to think a deer
Might catch me in her sight.

I don't know why she feared me so;
I'm happy to share my space.
Perhaps she had one time been trained
To be wary of my face.

For sure, I'd never hurt a deer.
I only stopped to stare
At the beauty of the moment
As I came out for some air.

And now she may lay somewhere hurting
Or frightened once again.
If only I had stopped to think
After putting down my pen.

We Are Climbers, All

MY DEAR, DO NOT LAY HURTING — Part II

Tonight, I think My Dear was hurt,
As I read her what I'd written
About a person long ago
With whom I once was smitten.

'Twas just a stream of consciousness,
A memory from the past
That found its way into my mind,
So I stopped and wrote it fast.

Then, thinking I could share the piece
Without causing any pain,
I read that poem to My Dear,
But my thinking was in vain.

It evoked in her some sullenness,
And anger I could see.
Perhaps she had one time been trained
To not place trust in me.

It's all my fault, I realize;
Some things are best not shared.
I guess I thought the poem benign,
But she looked at me and stared.

Much like that frightened, skittish deer,
As I walked into our field,
My Dear felt like she had to run
From hurts yet to be healed.

I simply wanted to share my art,
Not cause her such alarm.
If only she could realize
I truly meant no harm.   (concludes on next page)

Tom Blaisse

MY DEAR, DO NOT LAY HURTING — Part II
(conclusion)

And now she may lay somewhere hurting
Or frightened once again.
If only I had stopped to think
After putting down my pen.

And so I write this apology,
As I stare into the night.
My Dear, I pray you'll not stay hurting,
For everything's all right.

We Are Climbers, All

COMMON CENTS

I see both sides; it does makes sense,
The head and tail of a single pence.
"In God We Trust" and "One from Many."
I see both sides of that single penny.

Fresh from the mint, it glints for spite.
Then try as it might to stay upright,
It stumbles through a rally of years,
And fumbles through this valley of tears.

The date wears old, the luster fades.
Worth only half now? Ha'penny, trade?
Or, toss a wish into the drink.
Watch it sink, quick as a wink?

No!

It doubles as the date wears old.
Must not be tossed, dare not be sold.
For when we gray, it's here to stay.
Then how much more it will outweigh
Its weight in Gold.

CHAPTER THREE
On Living

We Are Climbers, All

THE MIRACLES OF LIFE

The Miracles of Life
Occur most every day.
Sometimes we don't take notice,
As we rush along our way.

The Miracles of Life
Can appear at any turn.
They drop in, just like angels.
They help us all to learn.

The Miracles of Life
Are like a child's toy:
Sometimes they are forgotten;
When found, they bring lost joy.

The Miracles of Life
Show up when least expected.
The answers that they give us
Are better than projected.

The Miracles of Life
Can help us climb each hill.
They're not within our power;
From God they shine at will.

Tom Blaisse

LITTLE KIDS

Little kids are like the Sun:
   They shine so bright all day.
They love to laugh and just have fun.
They teach us how to play.

Little kids are like the Moon:
   Silver in the night.
They always hum a happy tune.
They always feel what's right.

Little kids are like the Rain:
   Refreshing thirsty soil.
They keep us living, keep us sane.
They are forever loyal.

Little kids are like a Star:
   Sparkling up above.
They glimmer new, so like a car
That's just been buffed with love.

We Are Climbers, All

Little kids are like the Snow:
   Falling from the sky.
On their blankets they will go,
It's time for a lullaby.

Little kids are like a Tree:
   Someday they will grow tall.
But they will not forget to see
The fun of being small.

Little kids are like the Earth,
   God's natural resource.
Twice their weight in gold they're worth.
They grow up in due course.

Little kids will then have others,
   As God forever planned.
Little sisters, little brothers,
To love throughout the land.

Tom Blaisse

A DIRECTOR'S NOTE

AUDITIONS BEGIN; THE STAGE IS SET.
TO THE SCRIPT, I MUST BE TRUE.
    WHO BEST SAYS LINES?
    WHO FEELS THE PART?
WHO READS WITH PASSION AND GETS CALLED BACK?
THEN WHEN IT'S TIME, I WILL DECIDE
WHOM I WILL CHOOSE TO PLAY THE LEAD.

WHEN THE CAST IS SET, THE FRACTURE HEALS.
THE CHOICE WILL MAKE IT WORK.
    THEN WITH EVERY PRACTICE,
    UNTIL OPENING NIGHT,
I'LL PLAY THE PLAY THE WAY THAT'S RIGHT.
THINK NEVER OF WHAT MIGHT HAVE BEEN,
DECISIONS MADE WILL NEED TO STAY.

I MUST DIRECT, BE NOT DIRECTED;
BE MUTE, BUT BE NOT DUMB;
    MOVE THE SCENE,
    TRUST THE SCRIPT.
PACE THE RHYTHM, AND PHRASE THE LINES.
IF PASSION IS THERE, THEN ART WILL COME.
THE CRITIC'S RAVE WILL NOT BE FOR NAUGHT.

CATCH THE CONSCIENCE OF MY KING.
BE STILL AND LISTEN; THE PLAY'S THE THING.

We Are Climbers, All

THE CHESS GAME

The Move is not the final touch;
'Tis a stroke of thought;
    A single spark, briefly lighted,
That, fairly weighed
    And thus aligned with playing space,
Calls in silence when the tension swells.

The Move is not the victor's win.
'Tis a brief parlay,
    An inching itch, onetime echoed,
That, rightly armed
    And so well versed in marching step,
Mounts in grandeur when the power climbs.

The Move is not the finished scene
'Tis the brush's stroke;
    A single swipe, lonely sounded,
That, finely hued
    And tuned for balance with its art,
Marks in stillness when the vision clears.

The Move is not the total song.
'Tis a single note;
    A checking choice, first desired,
That, justly honored
    And placed so keenly in the measure,
Sings in accord when the spirit soars.

Tom Blaisse

OR WHAT'S A HEAVEN FOR?

Our reach should always exceed our grasp,
    Or "what's a heaven for?"
Our anticipation of what might be
    Is often loftier than what unfolds;
Our vision may surpass results.

If speed of light cannot be reached,
    Perhaps we can come close.
Our needs propel us to believe.
    Beliefs then spring us into action.
Our actions keep our dreams alive.

We might accept the incongruence
    With what sparked us to commit.
Yet knowing nothing's ever perfect,
    We thus mature, to strive again
For higher depths that exceed our grasp.

The Heaven we might find in Life
    Comes from our earthly climb.
Each mile reveals a smile gained;
    Each year conceals a tear of growth.
Each pause congeals the cause for faith.

With Hope, a failure we cannot be,
    Unless we do not learn.
For in the learning, we fuel desire;
    And with desire, we persist.
And with persistence, we succeed.

We Are Climbers, All

Yet some may say our sights seem silly,
    And we should change our course.
But we can trust the Light of God
    Will show the way at His own speed,
If we stay upon the Righteous Path.

Pitfalls and stumbles may be many,
    All haunting us to halt.
Rewards outweigh the labor spent.
    But when our weary bones need rest,
There will be room then at the inn.

The impact we have made in Life
    Will forge a path for all.
With love, we'll live in harmony.
    As long as there is Light to learn,
We'll seek, or "what's a heaven for?"

Tom Blaisse

THE CANDLE FLAME

The candle flame is like the Trinity:

The First Stage is the Earthly Root,
   Where life begins; its base is firm.
      'Tis the Father Figure begetting Word,
         That stems the wick and holds the fuel.
            A steady stream in the whistling wind,
               Its core is solid with a hollow heat.
                  It touches ground; brings life to light.

The Middle Stage is the Fire Tunnel,
   The Saving Grace that stretches Love.
      'Tis the knowing Soul, the Son of Man,
         That softly sees with floral lids.
            A see-through glaze, connecting Lives
               With warmth of centered openness,
                  It resurrects to divining dawn.

The Third Stage is the Rising Tip,
   That reaches up with forward flow.
      'Tis the Aura Peak, the Paraclete,
         That answers calls and guides the lost.
            A shadow shining alone in Virtue,
               This circling Spirit wakes one to Self.
                  It prances, dances; breathes in Art.

The Flame itself is wholly merged,
   From separate slices of single Beauty.
      'Tis endless, lilting, pure illumined,
         That spreads its power from standing straight.
            What might be hidden becomes aglow.
               If it be smothered, there is another
                  Kept burning brightly, this Candle Flame.

We Are Climbers, All

THE PRODUCTIVITY PYRAMID

What's Important? I must assess.
        How has my Time been spent?
Not quite sure, I must confess;
        The years just came and went.

The foundation I must lay in first,
        Each block to firmly fit.
Values calling, a deepening thirst,
        For strength to harbor wit.

What purpose am I to manifest?
        What reason for it all?
I crave to build, to be my best,
        Accept my mission's call.

The next step, then, is long-range goals,
        To bridge the values gap;
The Challenge of Change to pay Life's Tolls,
        A specific, measurable map.

Break down the goals before I start;
        Each step along the way;
I'll spend my Time working SMART,
        To see results some day.

Through daily tasks, I will produce.
        Distractions I'll resist.
Time Robbers I will, now, reduce;
        Success, if I persist.

I'll be content with what I've done;
        Productive days increase.
To balance work with a little fun
        Will nurture Inner Peace.

Tom Blaisse

JUST DO IT!

Still too busy with busi-ness,
    Racing toward tomorrow,
    Slipping in the sand,
    Refusing needed discipline,
    Dissipating energy?

Still too fearful, not fearless,
    Fleeing from the dragon,
    Hiding in the sheets,
    Making up excuses,
    Worrying about the dream?

Still too thoughtful, yet thoughtless,
    Hoping for beginnings,
    Praying in a sieve,
    Thinking more than doing,
    Veering off the target?

Stop the cycle! Change the path!
Set the goal! Ignore the wrath!
Take the time to contemplate.
Make the plan and activate.
Illusive Inner Peace will come.

RENEWAL

I feel as if I've been renewed.
    I had lost the taste of innocence;
    Had walled my thoughts upon themselves,
    Into a hollow tube of dullness.

But a spark of passion lived there still;
    I found the fuel to fondle warmth.
    With air to breathe, a fire stirred,
    And now burns brightly, lightly, there.

Some thoughts are cheerful when the stage is dark,
    To ponder answers upon which to perch.
    But thoughts grow sullen on a bleaker set,
    'Til doubt and fear inhibit life.

Thoughts and feelings can survive;
    A balance, then, for which to strive,
    Allowing both to stay alive,
    So Body, Mind, and Soul can thrive.

What pried me open? The new career?
    Yes, and joy of family life.
    I found renewal in Form and Substance,
    The shock of folly finding Truth.

A life once lost where longing had lain,
    Express I now a reborn spirit
    That smiles as if the world is new.
    I hear the meaning in what is here.

How long may I live? I cannot say.
    I'll share each moment, day by day.
    And with myself, I'll no longer feud.
    I feel as if I've been renewed.

Tom Blaisse

WE ARE CLIMBERS, ALL

If our dream is to touch the sky,
  Then the mountain poses a great challenge.
    There is no lift, no plane to ride.
      We are not birds that soar and perch,
        Nor spirit alone, to escape the gravity.

For our humanity hurts with every step.
  It scrapes and bruises, makes us slip and grab.
    Seeing not the crystal cap distracts our courage,
      The pebbles tumble; for how long it smarts!
        We fear the fall, yet chance the move ahead.

Hold steady,
  For the reign of terror comes up short.
    Now, toe again!
      The knot holds firm as we swing the height,
        And our aching joy transcends the joyous ache.

We Are Climbers, All

No heads look up, but kiss the ledge,
  Until when the flatland reached,
    The final pull, no further holds,
      The goal alone injects the needed strength
        To leap on top and dance in air.

We cannot tame the surge
  That floods the soul with heaven.
    No passion burns deeper;
      No flower smells sweeter;
        No star burns brighter
          Than the unsurpassed love
            We climbers embrace.

For to look up once and then look down
  Is everything that life can give.
    And when the scratches heal, the gladness swells,
      And the dream becomes alive.

COMMENTARIES

WHAT MAKES PEOPLE LEARN?..............................Page 3

STRUCTURE
This poem is very simple and unstructured, almost terse in its message. It has no obvious rhyme scheme nor verse format (except for the last verse). The piece encourages the reader to allow his or her thoughts to roam in different directions around a few key themes; i.e., Death, Love, and Life. The cascading format of each section's six nouns, which serve to define further those three themes, is more for visual effect than for context or meaning. The title is repeated in Line 1 of each section to remind the reader of the necessary question. Then the descriptive nouns answer that question around the respective themes. The conclusion verse offsets the cascading structure and serves as a summary spot, highlighting the final message of the piece. It is in "free verse" form to allow the simplicity of the two sentences to take hold. A condition identifies choice; suggests room to grow, and motivates change.

IMAGERY
Each word in the poem encourages a different image. The reader is invited to imagine the condition that might exist from each noun, and to reflect on how that condition might serve to stimulate someone to learn. Each noun can be interpreted as it is stated, or can be pondered with the reader relating his or her own experiences to it. The starkness of each noun suggests that there is no need to clarify the situation that is being suggested; it stands alone. The final verse emphasizes the opportunity for these conditions to "open up one's eyes," and face the "reality...of choice."

THEMES
It is said that the "layman's" definition of insanity is "doing the same thing and expecting different results." If we don't learn, we don't change. If we don't change, we are stuck with the same results. The themes of Death and Love suggest two opposites; Life invites a choice between the two. In the concluding verse, the word "Punctuates" serves as a strong action verb that suggests a practical opportunity for learning, splitting the difference between "what is and what could be" and filling the gap between the two. The last line suggests that we all have the "Freedom to Choose" not only how we will learn, but also what condition we create to motivate that learning.

PERSONAL COMMENT
As a Training & Development industry professional, I focus daily on ways to help people learn. This opening piece was not the first poem that I wrote, but I chose it to open this book because of its simplicity and brevity. As an introduction to the "Learning" chapter, it serves simply to set the reader in motion. It is the only poem in the book that has no traditional verse format. I purposely wrote it that way just to be different and also to allow its stark structure to underscore the conciseness of its content. As you'll see throughout this book, my usual style as a poet is more traditional, verse-oriented, with metered lines and rhyme schemes as deemed necessary. This poem is simply a "stream of consciousness" piece that remains almost exactly the same as when I wrote it.

Tom Blaisse

REALITY: CHECK IT OUT..............................Page 4

STRUCTURE
This poem tells the story of a high school assembly at which the main character, a teenage girl in the audience, shares her thoughts as the presentation unfolds. The 12 verses are 4 lines each, not necessarily in strict iambic tetrameter, but loosely fitting into four "feet," some of which start with a downbeat, some with an upbeat (i.e., DUM-di versus di-DUM). The choices were random and scattered, with no intended pattern. The female "persona" who's sharing her thoughts mixes echoing direct lines from the "teacher" (the on-stage presenter) with her attitudes about the points he is making, to questions she might be asking herself along the way. The first eight verses put forth strong negative attitudes toward the assembly presentation message. Then, beginning with Verse 9, her attitude turns around a bit, as she starts to identify some truth in the message and the possible impact that positive change might have in (her) life. The last few verses build on that positive attitude and desire to change, culminating in a resolution to "check out who I want to be, [a]nd create my own reality."

IMAGERY
As the "story" unfolds, there are multiple visual, auditory, and kinesthetic images that are clear and relatable. Imagine a group of 30–40 teenagers, sitting in small assembly room, wearing headphones, with rainbow hair, body piercings, doodle pads, and a strong and sometimes vocal desire to get it over with and an urgency to go back to doing nothing. Because the style is "stream of consciousness," the images are simple and short, darting quickly in and out of each verse. In Verse 7, "red lights flashing" and "band-aids" allude to metaphors for a call to change covered up with a short-term fix.

THEMES
There is much denial early in the piece, until Verse 9, when the girl (author) shifts after realizing that a negative attitude leads to negative feelings, actions, and results. To achieve a positive result in one's life, one must begin with a positive attitude, followed by positive feelings, and actions. That is reality; check it out.

PERSONAL COMMENT
As indicated in this poem's byline, I wrote it from the perspective of a "troubled teen" being challenged to change. In the early '90s, I conducted an assembly for a group of high school students with a history of behavioral and emotional problems. Much of the content was borrowed from the "Reality Model" used in the FranklinCovey Co. *Stress Management* seminar. The model is based on Cognitive Therapy, and can be used to help people identify irrational beliefs that are driving inappropriate or unproductive behaviors that "may not meet one's needs over time." I vividly recall one female student coming up to me after that assembly, to thank me for helping her see the need for some changes in her life. Perhaps she was the only one in the audience who "got it." I wrote this poem from her perspective, combining attitudes and behaviors from many teenagers in that assembly, distilling them down to her persona.

We Are Climbers, All

LEARNING THROUGH LOVE .... Page 6

STRUCTURE
The first three verses focus on negative motivators: sin, pain, and fear, all of which can cause people to learn; the fourth verse proposes that we all best learn through love. After posing their initial question, each verse presents specific examples of that given condition. Obviously, there is no rhyme scheme in this poem, but the first line of each verse is written in iambic* trimeter. Then, Lines 2–5 in each verse (which are indented to set them apart from each Line 1) include a strong action verb, to describe what someone might be actually doing to create the condition (of sin, pain, or fear).

*An iamb is a double beat that sounds like di-DUM. If there were five iambs, the rhythm would be iambic pentameter (used primarily in Shakespeare's blank verse).

IMAGERY
The opening lines set up the main images for each verse: pain, sin, fear, love. The other lines use the action verbs to set up the activity, followed by the actual condition that is being created by that verb: to slip and slide; and force; to laugh; then cry. Each verb establishes a reason for the condition to exist. The conditions are vivid and purposefully uncomfortable. **Verse 1**: fields of dung; dirt upon our brows; iniquities; deeds foreclosed. **Verse 2**: stony faults; broken backs; anger and malcontent; suffering sands. **Verse 3**: shallow water holes; stands erect; feeling no faith; shattered haven (an oxymoron). **Verse 4** then shifts to positive imagery: above the earth; God disciples us; Courage…calming state; Love's embrace. The emotional impact of the poem is enhanced by the power of the above visual and kinesthetic images.

THEMES
There are many ways to learn—through sin, pain, or fear, with love being the most fulfilling and God-centered. **Verse 1** suggests that "Sin" can be playful (in dung) like a little kid painting his/her face with "dirt," laughing at first, but then crying at the realization that it has all been in vain ("deeds foreclosed"). **Verse 2** sets up physical and emotional "pain" and the subsequent futility of it all ("stony faults," " broken back," "malcontent" "suffering sands"). Similarly, **Verse 3** identifies fearful behaviors (creeping, hiding, falling, seeking). **Verse 4** uses strong words to underscore conditions of Love (Lift our souls, God disciple us, Courage, breeze, embrace). How we learn becomes a habitual pattern in our lives that can produce great discord, pain, or fear. Or, we can learn by tapping in on a pattern of Love, from God, from and for each others. The choice, of course, is always our own. But the question still remains.

PERSONAL COMMENT
This is one of my favorite poems, not just because of its message and philosophy, but because of it format and style. Utilizing a strong structure with vivid imagery and discernible themes, the piece is easy to read. But it calls the reader to read it again; to ponder, and to reflect how he or she may learn along the path of life.

TALENT .... Page 7

STRUCTURE
This poem has five verses. The first three set up strong metaphors for talent; the last verse is somewhat didactic in its approach. The final line is "preachy" in that it encourages the reader to think carefully about using one's talent or "be sad." Although Verses 1–4 vary in their meter, they are somewhat formal and consistent. Each verse begins with a metaphor. Then lines 2–4 of each verse further explain how and why the metaphor works and its application in the world. Verse 5 changes it up by removing the metaphors and getting to the point. Note also the purposeful use of capital letters for some of the nouns and verbs, used to invite the reader to extend the context beyond the obvious comparison, and to view Talent in more universal context.

IMAGERY
The metaphors set up the imagery of each of the first five verses, using key words:
- **Verse 1:** God's gift, refinement (of the Mind), buried; (coupled with) desire;
- **Verse 2:** nature, energy, unchallenged, search;
- **Verse 3:** bell, rung (auditory image), unanswered, (can't be) ignored;
- **Verse 4:** (visual and kinesthetic images): lies (within us) lose, to work, play, think—(examples of) creative expression…an attitude toward the world.

The final sentence contrasts action with a negative emotional feeling. Because Talent can come in so many forms, the metaphors used and the images created from them allow for a very vivid reading of this poem.

THEMES
Similar to Bible's New Testament story of the men who were given varying numbers of "talents," so it is with "God's Gifts." We need to pray for the "desire" to use our talents, and "explore" opportunities to develop and apply them. Verse 1 implies a "first nature" if Talent is our "second nature." The former might suggest a lack of awareness, laziness, or even indifference; the latter implies energy, challenge, and finding through searching. Verse 3 clearly "rings true," that talent is "silent until…rung." We might, for some time, try to ignore the "call," but eventually we must answer it. Verse 4 again alludes to a Bible story: "Faith is like a mustard seed"—a very small seed that grows into a very large tree. A simple talent, with faith, can move mountains and create fertile soil to foster its growth. Verse 4 encourages us to use our talent as a tool for manifesting "purpose" in our lives. Talent can take on many forms, as proven by Reality TV shows like *America's Got Talent*. It can be as simple as an attitude. Creative Expression is life lived in Love.

PERSONAL COMMENT
I believe that the gifts (talents) endowed upon us by our Creator grant us not only the opportunity but also the responsibility to use them to benefit mankind. We need to develop them over time and seek ways to share them with others, otherwise we "hide our light under a bushel."

THE CHALLENGE OF CHANGE .... Page 8

STRUCTURE
The poem is really two poems in one: A reader could perceive a complete message from just the first six verses (of three lines each) and end with that, or read only the last four verses (of four lines each) as a complete thought. Verses 1–3 each set up a one-sentence question of Change, beginning with "Can someone..." followed repeatedly by "And...." Lines 1 and 2 of Verses 1–3 are all iambic trimeter, with each verse's Line 3 wrapping it up with iambic tetrameter. Verses 4–6 proclaim a resounding "Yes!" to the questions posed by each earlier verse. The iambic meter varies with the need of each line, with the last word in Verses 4 and 5 rhyming, followed by a rhyming couplet in Verse 6. Verses 4–6 support the "Yes!" and offer specific direction to the reader on what to change, and why. These last four verses are quatrains with no rhyme scheme. Lines 1, 2, and 4 are in iambic trimeter, and each verse's Line 3 is in iambic tetrameter.

IMAGERY
Verse 1 begins with a sense of movement ("from then to now") underscored by the need to "break a mold." **Verse 2** contains the action verbs "lift" and "forge," and **Verse 3** uses "reconstruct" an "angry" (list) followed by (a paradox) "productive stress." **Verses 4–6** set forth that one's purpose needs to be "solid in the heart," followed by the proverbial "sights...raised" and "soul" being "moved" (to start.) The brevity of the rhyming couplet strengthens both the "sure" resolve and "pure" intention. The "second half" of the poem includes action images such as "wisdom grows," "fruits of patience seen," virtue plowed," and "flat and weak." **Verse 9**, which uses the colorful image and metaphor of the butterfly, is a marvelous standalone verse.

THEMES
It's all about "Change," beginning with the questions posed in Verses 1–3, which remind the reader of the need to change "beliefs," break the old "mold," and let go of "anger." The strong affirmation of Verses 4–6 is conditional to the "solid...heart," raised "sights," leading to inner motivation ("soul...moved to start"), and then, again the rhyming couplet at the end. The resolution and command in Verses 7–10 emphasize both the justification to change as well as the direction to take so one can feel the freedom of accepting the challenge of change.

PERSONAL COMMENT
I wrote this very personal poem while I was a Seminar Leader with FranklinCovey Co. I was working with their "Reality Model," which suggests that our basic Human Needs (To Live, To Love and be Loved, Variety, and To Feel Important) drive beliefs on our "Belief Window" that lead us to follow "Rules" of "Behavior" that impact "Results." The existential question posed is then "Will the result of my (your) behavior meet my (your) needs over time?" (See the "Reality: Check It Out" poem.) Serving on a team that was creating a new "Personal Change" workshop gave me the impetus to write this poem.

Tom Blaisse

Dear God... Page 10

STRUCTURE
As a prayer, this poem is a "stream of consciousness" piece, and therefore is more free-form than most. The five verses were not meant to be similar in format, however, in its revised version, there is more structure than in its original state. Verses 1, 2, 3, and 5 contain three indented phrases: Verse 1 poses a few existential questions; and the other three verses contain several specific petitions to the Almighty. Note the repetition of the words in the indented phrases in Verses 1, 2, and 5. The parallel structure in Verse 4 is underscored by the use of the three strong "E" action verbs.

IMAGERY
Strong images permeate the piece:
- **Verse 1:** heart be spared; weather the tempest; peace inject me; hurled into the light of Your Love;
- **Verse 2:** embrace...warmth; alone followed by three antonyms: darkness...light, abyss...foundation, loss...hope;
- **Verse 3:** trust...waning; eyes...closed, the three "E" action verbs and the (visual, auditory and kinesthetic) images: see...eyes, hear...ears, feel...strength;
- **Verse 4:** a standalone segment with very strong allusions: love...cries out; will to grow; world of weeds. "Passion" can be interpreted either negatively (burden) or positively (joy), then it asks who might be the recipient;
- **Verse 5:** begins with a plea (hold...here; thoughts call up), then suggests an "Aha!" moment (of recognition), followed by three more petitions and strong images (Truth...Word, Bread...Life, Win...Salvation), ending with "Joy...finally found." A paraphrase of Shakespeare's line, "Winter of my discontent" becomes "bask in the Summer of my contentment."

THEMES
Life is difficult, and is best "weathered" with God's love supporting us. During dark times, when one feels out of control, peace, love, warmth, and understanding emerge with an "injection" of "acceptance." The reader might be reminded of "The Serenity Prayer": "Lord, grant me the serenity to accept the things I cannot change; the courage to change the things I can; and the wisdom to know the difference." After weathering the tempest, and bearing the burden—and the joy—of passion, we resurrect enlightened, energized, and empowered.

PERSONAL COMMENT
I wrote this very personal and reflective poem many years ago, during a "dark" period in my life, when things weren't going well. The piece is plaintive in form and yet affirming in substance. It is certainly a prayer, somewhat childlike in its approach, yet clearly mature in its style and language. Even though I have revised the poem with some minor word or thought changes, and made it a bit more structured, the main "message" to the Creator is the same: "Lord, give me the strength daily to continue to 'climb my mountain' (for you)."

We Are Climbers, All

EVENING PRAYERS.. Page 11

STRUCTURE
As a first-person narrative, the poem is direct and simple, with six similar verses formatted in parallel structure. Each verse has five lines, with Lines 2 and 3 indented. There is no iambic rhythm and no rhyme scheme, nor any attempt to repeat the cadence of each line from one verse to the next. The piece is "stream of consciousness," which was only later formatted in the editing. It is made up of two equal halves: Verses 1–3 set up the situation from childhood; what was happening, and the innocence of it all. Verses 4–6 flip to adulthood, with a reflection on what is *now* compared to what was *then*. Each verse is a complete thought in its own, building on the one before it, and opening the way for the verse after it.

IMAGERY
Picture words and action verbs create vivid images that empower the reader to feel the tone of it. **Verse 1** creates the scene quickly: new...fresh; attached; kneeling nightly at the household hamper. **Verse 2** injects some feeling around the scene: suspicion by big sister; in peace...He [is] there, above the...clothes. **Verse 3** suggests some solitude, serenity, and simplicity: privacy of thought; clairvoyance; praying prettily; curves...ahead; perfect dream. **Verse 4** quickly makes the shift (since then) and paints a few Shakespearean-style metaphors (thoughts collect as dew that dries past dawn....unarmed except by faith), with the return to a child's state without need of a hamper for protection. **Verse 5:** speak in softness...sharper tongue; servant...fed in innocence. **Verse 6:** darkness...surrender; thoughts...bequeathed; with strength, endurance, courage...bow...hamper none. Using the word "hamper" now as a verb, not a noun, changes the imagery and the meaning.

THEMES
The theme of childhood is innocence coupled with newness and unbridled faith. Adulthood can bring doubt ("sifted thoughts [that] collect as dew that dries past dawn") coupled with a desire to return to an "unhampered" childlike state. As adults, we can know that God, as our Father, can and will still listen to His servants' pleas. We may have known the darkness, but we can surrender and become re-attached (betrothed) to God.

PERSONAL COMMENT
I can't get more personal than with this poem. It is autobiographically honest and simple. Yes, I did pray at the family hamper when I was a preschooler. And yes, big sister (who helped me edit this book) did look askance at me while I was so doing. Perhaps I was still scared of the dark, or just didn't want to be in the hallway during my nighttime prayers. But as I reflect back, I am aware that the innocence of my early childhood was fueled by faith, hope, and love for God, family, and self. As a "grown-up," I find it easy to forget that "age of innocence." And yet we are taught to come to God as a Child might—awestruck, eager, and full of wonder. "Not my will but Thine be done."

Tom Blaisse

TO THE TEACHER .... Page 12

STRUCTURE
Each of the four verses in this poem follow the same structure: Lines 1, 2, and 4 are iambic trimeter; Line 3 is iambic tetrameter. The rhyme scheme is an atypical ABCB. As with many very structured verses, this poem could lend itself to a tune, except perhaps that the theme is a bit too ponderous. Verses 1–3 set up challenges for a teacher (indeed, for the world), with each verse beginning with "In the..." followed by "When...," then "And...." Note that these three verses are single sentences that build on each other, connected with semicolons. The end of Verse 3 has a colon that sets up Verse 4, to reconcile all the challenges with a classic homage to the teacher for his/her efforts and results. Given it's a strict meter, it is important to read the poem with a prosaic style, de-emphasizing the obvious rhyme and rhythm of the piece.

IMAGERY
The beauty of this poem is in the richness of the images created for the reader in every line. One can see, hear, or feel the impressions made with each idea presented. Note the picture and feeling words:
    Verse 1: Indecisions, split apart, joy...safe, solid in the heart (all very kinesthetic);
    Verse 2: Growing wonderment; confusion, twisted, dead (emotionally gut-wrenching);
    Verse 3: Work...forever, (can't be) found, turn...heads, tearful, fearful frowns (visual and emotional)
    Verse 4: Note the action verbs beginning each phrase, followed by a strong visual or emotional image: (Surpass) gory doubt, (Finger through) the mire, (Lighten up) so many minds, (Cultivate) desire.

THEMES
The message in this poem is that the world is a pretty frightening place, falling apart, decelerating over time. One would think all is lost, but No! The teacher is there to break through the "doubt" and the "mire," and to once again "cultivate desire." The overtones of this poem suggest a teacher's mission is one of worldly or even spiritual salvation.

PERSONAL COMMENT
I wrote this poem in 1983, as a birthday card to my mentor who was the owner of Asset Center/Wilson Learning of Philadelphia, a small training and consulting firm. Back then, I felt I had finally found my niche, as a Seminar Leader and Adult Learning Facilitator. The "boss" taught me a lot about working a classroom, and using the "self-discovery" adult learning method. The original title of this poem was "To The Trainer." I later re-titled it "To The Teacher," having realized that the job of a teacher/trainer is indeed not only a most formidable one but also a most rewarding one. This poem is on a plaque hanging in my office, to remind me of my Mission: "Turning on lights so people can shine."

MY DEAR CHILD..Page 15

STRUCTURE
With three short verses and a final closing line, this poem is somewhat terse and to the point. Each verse repeats the first line, to remind the reader of the main message, followed by three more examples of how God will "haunt" us. Each line begins with "I will..." suggesting that the statement is God's commitment to us, not just an article of faith. All of the "I will" lines promise an action, mostly positive, and all of which are beneficial to our well-being and redemption. There is no need for a rhyme scheme; the repetition of the format creates its own rhythm, and the images bring out a peaceful harmony. The signature line "As Always" underscores the infinite nature of God's love and parental affection for humankind.

IMAGERY
The repeatable "haunt" for the "good of you within" is a paradox in that we usually think of "haunt" as something bad or to be feared. This poem proposes that because we are "good...within," God will "haunt" us with His gifts and encouragements. Each action word is followed by a further clarification or reason for that promise.

Verse 1: mystify...wildest imagination; greet...smiles, ever; pardon...you...wish it.
Verse 2: rescue...drowning in despair; cast out...demons...anger; love...(lost) child...found.
Verse 3: nurture and enrich...starving; praise and admonish...deeds and...conceit; grant...desires; faith...effort.
Verse 4: welcomed home....paradise (suggesting an embrace from the arms of our Creator).

THEMES
God is a god of promise and traditional covenant. He provides for us out of a sense of fatherly duty and loyalty. (S)he counsels us with a motherly insight and assuredness. The "parental" theme permeates throughout this poem, with a flavor of "tough love" and sustainability that only a loving, committed parent can provide. Without looking ahead at the end line signature, the reader might expect that the poem might be written by a parent to his/her own child. And yet there is a supernatural overtone (mystify, pardon, rescue, cast out, grant desires) that foreshadows the signature and allows the reader to think, "Oh yes, of course, this is God talking to me."

PERSONAL COMMENT
I don't recall the exact motivation behind this poem, or the time of its writing, but it comes from my imagining how God might respond to us as His Children. I use the word "haunt" in a positive vein, as in "The music had a haunting melody"—one that stays with you after hearing it. And because God believes that we are inherently "good," He commits to staying with us in our time of need.

YOU ARE GOOD ....Page 16

STRUCTURE
The four short verses of this poem are more about clever word usage than deep meaning. Similar to the "We Are Family" poem, Line 1 of each verse repeats the title. Lines 2–4 of each verse give, and are followed by, three separate examples of "good" used as metaphors for the person being addressed. Each of those three lines in each verse is written in strict iambic trimeter, and begin with "As a [noun]...," with obvious inner rhymes (action verbs) ending with a bold AAA rhyme scheme.

IMAGERY
The brevity of each line helps each image come out clearly and simply. Several are visual images: eye...light; day...night; smile....told; book....old. Some are kinesthetic or intellectual images: mind...right; dream...thought; coach....taught; breeze...naught; hug...cold; heart...song; love...wrong; soul...strong.

THEMES
Many people believe that human nature, though flawed, is basically good. If we look at someone as "good," we can compare that goodness to many other things in life that are also good, whether they be in nature, in the decisions we make, or in how we perceive and receive things that come our way. Almost all of the metaphors in the poem unfold as they do without corruption or manipulation. They seem obvious, and each suggests a feeling of innocence. Exceptions might be "As a breeze resumes for naught," which suggests a gentle breeze coming back for no apparent reason than to comfort on a hot day. The other metaphors are more self-evident.

PERSONAL COMMENT
Although I have no recollection of what prompted the writing of this poem, at first glance, this simple piece might seem a bit silly, even inane. As mentioned in the Structure section above, I wrote it more as an exercise in clever word usage than with the intention to purport a sublime message. However, upon further reading (beyond the cute rhymes and propitious metaphors), the images seem to support the main argument of the poem that "You Are Good...As a....." Therefore, the metaphors hold up nicely in each line of the poem. Would that we could be so good in reality.

We Are Climbers, All

IT DOESN'T WORK .... Page 17

STRUCTURE
The poem contains four verses of six lines each. There is no rhyme scheme, but it is shaped with a very precise iambic tetrameter meter. The first line in Verses 1–3 begins with the same opener (To pass on a hurt just doesn't work), and then further explains the reason why that is so (in the five indented lines). Verse 4 then turns around the message "To forgive a hurt is what does work" and also explains why.

IMAGERY
This "artsy" piece contains images that may need a second reading to understand fully. Many of the coupling phrases throughout the poem use words that usually don't go together:
- **Verse 1:** shallow fortress; baseless hold;
- **Verse 2:** dampness swells; solid bars fall soft…; hurt springs back;
- **Verse 3:** swampy sadness; pervades the muck; no beams leak out; no joy is born; braces tight;
- **Verse 4:** rise above to loosen the bonds; bar the healing from seeping through.

Other colorful images include "Pain unceasing…ever growing," replacing "pain" with "joy" in the last line of the poem. Then "protect…hides; slip, then sink…deeper down." And because the end does not justify the means, "returns diminish." Then "escape the torment;" and lastly, "truth…courage; clouds lifted; freedom reigns." In Verse 1, Pain is personified, to suggest "it" "fronts…a strength; cannot protect…hides; cannot serve to patch the sores."

THEMES
The key theme is that forgiveness will always trump revenge (which is passing on a hurt to another) because it is stronger and much more rewarding long term (joy unceasing….). Each of the first three verses present its own reasons why it doesn't work "to pass on a hurt" (weakness; sadness and sinking; lack of light). It takes courage to "loose the bonds," but when "freedom (from the hurt) reigns," the outcome is "joy unceasing…."

PERSONAL COMMENT
This poem states a philosophy consistent with the Natural Law of Reciprocity; i.e., we reap that which we sow. When one is holding on to or passing on a hurt, he/she is the one who is hurting the most. When I was a kid, my father used to encourage me to try to "rise above it," "let it go," or "don't let it drag you down." These truths do indeed set us free.

Tom Blaisse

ALL RELATIONSHIPS SERVE A PURPOSE.......... Page 18

STRUCTURE
Even before reading the words of this poem, the reader can see that it has a very tight structure and repetitive format. All six verses are alike in length and iambic meter. Obviously, the first line is reinforced as an introduction to each verse, followed by two somewhat opposing thoughts and a final summary line. Lines 1–3 of each verse are written in iambic tetrameter (with a few variations). Line 4 of each verse is in a simple iambic dimeter. The piece also has a unique rhyme scheme: Lines 2 and 3 of each verse rhyme, and all verses' Line 4 rhyme.

IMAGERY
The word choices are simple and clear, to allow images to emerge easily: mix...match; smart...tearing....apart; season...reason; smooth...edges...pull out...hue; grain...rain; plow...again; wondering hearts...cup full of Love...spiked with a tear; road....clear; roadblocks up...shove. Note in Verse 5 the paraphrase of Clement Clark Moore's poem "A Visit from St. Nicholas" (aka "'Twas the Night Before Christmas"). Also, the "o" rhyming words at the end of each verse's Line 4 (grow, flow, glow, sow, know, go) set up vivid pictures of their own along the way.

THEMES
The repeating first line drives the main theme home *ad infinitum*. Each verse takes a different point of view, justifying that opening theme with "ups and downs," which continues the *We Are Climbers, All* book theme, with this poem opening the "On Loving" chapter. Bottom line: Life would be pretty boring and unfulfilling without relationships. We can't live with them; we can't live without them. One could be reminded of the customer service employee who might have been overheard saying, "My job would be soooo much easier if it weren't for all these customers coming in all day!"

PERSONAL COMMENT
I believe this is one of the first poems I wrote many years ago (that found its way into the book). I was a young adult, feeling my way through the vicissitudes of life and discovering the impact that relationships were having on my life. The poem is a reflection on some of those relationships and the impact that they had on me. The piece is a bit whimsical, not too heavy, but rather breezy and simple. The tone of the poem is cute but not terribly pithy. I had fun writing it; more fun editing it, and I still have fun reading it.

We Are Climbers, All

OUR LOVED ONES.. Page 19

STRUCTURE
This poem could be another one of those "standalone" pieces, on a wall poster. As a five-verse narrative with a beginning, middle, and end, each verse is five lines, each in a combination of iambic trimeter or tetrameter. As a formatting choice, Line 2 and Line 5 in each verse are indented. There is no rhyme scheme, but note the four-word alliteration in Verse 4, at the end of Line 5 (...what was will win). The poem is written in the 2nd-person plural, to engage everyone in its message and to create an emotional response for the readers.

IMAGERY
Verse 1: Love and warmth often go together, and associating "names" with a "prayer" conjures a mystical image.
Verse 2 contains various visual, kinesthetic, and auditory images: touch...hands; faces gleam; voices...sparkle; journey's end.
Verse 3: wash...spot; change...memories; touch...spirits.
Verse 4: deny...truth; harbor...pain; icy chill; snow-capped...victory; beauty...win.
Verse 5: God...Time...free; Heaven's Gate; loved ones passing through; warm...souls.

THEMES
Love is eternal. The thoughts, feeling, and actions associated with "loved ones" seem to never die even long after their passing. They are in our lives as we grow older, perhaps more so as we near our own demise. It may be easier to dismiss that truth, and thus avoid the pain, especially initially. But over time, that pain transcends to joy and even anticipation. We seem to have both a spiritual and psychological need to stay connected. Maybe it's part of our human nature to want to believe that those we loved who have died are "somewhere" watching over us, and that we will see them again. It is comforting to believe that, and perhaps necessary to be reminded of it.

PERSONAL COMMENT
As with all of these poems, I wrote this loving piece many years ago, long before my own parents died. Until that time, the only taste of the loss from death was from my paternal grandparents. (My maternal grandparents both passed before I was age 5.) As I write this, it has been 12 years since my mother passed, and 2 years since my father passed. As a kid, I was taught to remember and pray for my "deceased" relatives and friends. I find it comforting and gratifying to continue to feel that love for them (and from them).

Tom Blaisse

WE ARE FAMILY..Page 20

STRUCTURE
With "book-end" verses repeating the title of the poem at the beginning and end of each verse, and five lines "sandwiched" in between, this poem follows a clear progression of community relationships, from families to spirits in heaven. Line 2 of each verse follows an iambic trimeter meter; opens the topic of the verse; and is followed by four "ing" descriptive lines, of iambic tetrameter, consisting of a simple AABB rhyme scheme. The last verse serves as a summary of all the verses before it.

IMAGERY
While Line 2 of each verse sets up the topic of that verse, the visual images emerge as the reader envisions them. Lines 3–6 of each verse introduce a plethora of additional images by way of the "ing" actions described.
    Visual: sharing, working, eating, saying (grace), helping, solving, giving, taking; praying, contributing, supporting, swapping, sharing (rides), sowing, tolerating, stopping (wars), giving (peace).
    Kinesthetic: laughing, crying, joining (forces), holding (hands).
    Olfactory: baking.

THEMES
The reader is reminded on one's connectedness to others in many groups, beginning with the basic unit of society, the family. We nurture and are nurtured by others in our own family, as well as in our neighborhoods, places of worship, companies, and countries. We engage in activities within these groups, to produce results and to support those in these various communities. As with a family, we are all different and have different needs, strengths, and responsibilities. In the end, we are all just spirits, made in the image of God, living a human existence, and viewed as equals in the eyes of our Creator.

PERSONAL COMMENT
I don't recall exactly when I wrote this poem (many years ago), but each time I read it, I am reminded of the universality of our human needs and desires. Psychology 101 tells us that us that all behavior stems from an attempt to meet our human needs. We become members of groups to meet the need for "Belongingness" (Abraham Maslow) and to "Love and Be Loved" (Stephen R. Covey). Ideally, our family creates a feeling of a loving, helping community, charged with a mission of collaboration and mutual benefit. So too should it be with all of our societal groups—teams with a win/win attitude and an abundance mentality.

We Are Climbers, All

AT THE FIRESIDE .... Page 22

STRUCTURE
The poem is a bit of an epic in that it tells a story of a fire kindled; nurtured; left to fade, and then reignited the next day. The 4 lines of each of the 10 verses are all written in strict iambic tetrameter. No rhyme scheme is present except for the couplet at the end. Occasional alliteration colors the cadence: stand shouting; triumphant trumpet; piques a purring…; leaps…love long lived; drowsiness does not drift in; fire flares; piece…puffed up; steam subsides; arise again. The story of the fire (and its analogy of an intimate relationship) is separated into two parts: Verses 1–5 set up the story, and Verses 6–10 find the "fire" dwindling and dying out, until restored the next morning.

IMAGERY
Strong images dominate the poem.
- **Visual—Part 1:** The fire igniting: wood…dressed in style; tips…come aglow; fire ghost; cradled what's newly born; flame to stretch; up and the down the fire flares…puffed up with air; watchful eyes…nourishment.
- **Visual—Part 2:** steam subsides…rainbow fades; fading stars…shunned by ash; clouds of smoke; twinkles dim; red poke through the gray; new fire…single ember.
- **Auditory—Part 1:** papers crumbled; crackling blitz; logs…stand shouting; blare a trumpet call; heat begins to speak.
- **Auditory—Part 2:** not a whistle can be heard; desires shouts….; flame…cries for more; boasts of joy.
- **Kinesthetic—Part 1:** air…joined with fuel; cold blue room; flame…haunts the soul…warmth; piques a purring; gentle breeze; vibrant heat; hunger; passion leaps; nourishment; drowsiness.
- **Kinesthetic—Part2:** one-time warmth…turns to cold; stay awake; sleeping time; blankets….surrogates; hope…love abides.

THEMES
This is an allegorical poem that tells of a personal relationship coming alive and nurtured with warmth and love, later being neglected and allowed to dwindle down and die out. The poem's happy ending is that the next day (or sometime later), the "fire" is rekindled. New relationships must be tended to regularly until they are burning brightly. Often they simply burn out from "lack of fuel." And then we wake up wondering what happened and try to bring them back to life—sometimes successfully; sometimes not.

PERSONAL COMMENT
I wrote this poem more than 30 years ago, long before I was married, as a testament to the demise of another long relationship (in my 20's) that had been fraught with turmoil off and on for a long time. After the final goodbye, I went back home and this piece spilled out. It occurred to me then that the "fire" analogy was appropriate, not only to my personal situation at that time, but that it was an apt metaphor for most types of intimate relationships and the type of journey they put us on.

A FAIR..Page 24

STRUCTURE
With three simple five-line verses in a repeatable flow of images that tell a story and carve a destiny, this poem needs no rhyme (or reason); it just is. A stream of consciousness piece perceived in its moment of reality: A carnival with all its smells and bells. To set up the series of images, the first four (tight iambic tetrameter) lines of each verse begin with "The...." and end with a considered conclusion. The similarity in the action verbs that start each verse's Line 5 (invites, incites, ignites) is a play on words consistent with the setting of "A Fair" or perhaps "An Affair." The many uses of alliteration are intended to keep the piece airy and light-hearted: stepping stones, scratching soles, sunny strokes, tire tread, smiling Smurf, waiting....win; freely flows; tempting touch...timely.

IMAGERY
By the very nature of the piece, each line of the poem presents a strong image that naturally flows from a carnival environment.
- **Visual:** sunny strokes; tire tread (on the muddy path); the doll...the smiling Smurf; (the girl); which ball to throw; life in altered form (married or single).
- **Auditory:** thrill of rides...glee (the reader might hear screams from the crowd on the ride) coupled with the "sound of winning not yet felt".
- **Kinesthetic:** "stepping stones on scratching soles"—Feeling the rough stones on the walkway, scratching against the soles (souls); "Work's impounded days" (the carnies had been stuck there all week, setting up the carnival.) Incites the mood; breezy talk...freely flows; thrill...rides....glee (double entendre); Temping touch; ignites a tacit, placid glow (a visual image also).
- **Olfactory:** grease and sweat; smell of food inviting taste (gustatory image).

THEMES
Underlying the entire piece of vivid memory is a subtle erotic theme that "incites the mood...," "invites a life...," and "ignites a...glow." The doll—the Smurf—is out there waiting to be won...as we wonder "which ball to throw." Beyond the carnival setting and the subtext of a romantic opportunity, one might interpret this poem to be saying that Life is like a fair (quite an affair) that requires balancing the "carnie sweat" with "the thrill of (the) ride's impending glee" (the physical and spiritual delights life includes).

PERSONAL COMMENT
Although it was close to 30 years ago, I can still put myself back there right now. The scene was a regional carnival with all the trimmings. We walked together, hand-in-hand for the first time, after being "friends" for several months. The physical distance between us (six hours by car) made it difficult to imagine a future, at least at first. But after several months of bi-monthly business trips, that reason had run its course, and I knew it was time to decide to let go; to feel or lose out. I considered this "life in altered form" and, believing that God's Will for our lives included each other, I won that "smiling Smurf" and married her a year later.

GARDEN FLOWER .... Page 25

STRUCTURE
Four simple, rhyming verses of four lines each make this poem another "standalone" piece that is focused and traditional. The format is iambic tetrameter; somewhat uneven at times, but with a steady four-beat rhythm that is pronounced in the reading of it. With a repetitive ABCB rhyme scheme, the poem "blossoms" as it progresses like a short story. First the reader notices the flower's wilting state, then ponders whether to care for it or let it melt in the frost; take it or in allow it stand in the wind. The final verse then decides the flower's fate and affirms its value.

IMAGERY
Verse 1 sets up the flower's condition: withered by "the currents of the Fall"; "survive unless downtrodden; "take it in?"
Verse 2 includes some strong visual, kinesthetic, and even olfactory images: pruned...fertilized...strength; untouched...melt into the frost.
Verse 3 uses "warm" as a verb as opposed to the usual adjective, followed by sharp visual and kinesthetic images: nurtured softness; wither out of place; wind to blow.
Verse 4: its own rebirth; reach out...share its life; love my flower for all its worth.

THEMES
The fourth verse confirms the suspected allegory of the piece; i.e., the flower is a loved one, full of worth. Be it a friend, spouse, parent, or child, the "flower" is best "left to find its own rebirth." The challenge with any loving relationship is how often to intervene; how often to watch it wither (with the frost). An additional theme might be that a figurative death can lead to a resurrection, a shared life when someone reaches out with love.

PERSONAL COMMENT
Each Fall, the flowers I have planted in my garden begin to fade and wither. One year, a certain lonely petunia (Oops, I gave it away!) seemed to be weathering the cooling nights and the morning frost. It was the only one left in the front garden and I felt sorry for it. I also felt somewhat ambiguous about its fate, struggling with my joyful memory of its glorious exponential blooming throughout the summer, now withered after having weathered the Fall, as I could see its impending death ahead. It occurred to me then that our loved ones are like flowers. And so this poem can be read with a double meaning. May you enjoy and appreciate your "flowers" while they are in bloom.

MY DEER, DO NOT LAY HURTING — PART I ......Page 26
MY DEAR, DO NOT LAY HURTING — PART II.....Page 27

STRUCTURE
As another epic piece, this poem tells a real story. Part 1 is about a scared deer running away from the house, back into the woods and then across the road. Part 2 tells about the author's "dear" (wife) who retreated, scared by his thoughtless gesture of sharing something personal he had written. Parts 1 and 2 each tell the story in 7 verses; Part 2 has two additional concluding verses. All the verses have four lines each. Lines 1 and 3 of each verse are written in iambic tetrameter; Lines 2 and 4 are in iambic trimeter. The rhyme pattern is ABCB throughout.

IMAGERY
As the story unfolds, vivid images allow the reader to see, hear, and feel what is happening in each line.
- **Part 1:** deer...hurt; jumped; leaped; squeal; surprised; spot it; looked both ways; humming; stepped...night; deer...catch me....; feared me; wary; beauty of the moment; some air; lay hurting.
- **Part 2:** dear...hurt; smitten; causing...pain; sullenness; stared; run...hurt yet healed; alarm; lay hurting; frightened; stare.

THEMES
Fear and insecurity can cause trepidation and the desire to flee. The deer was afraid by instinct; the "dear" perhaps by conditioning. Both became skittish when confronted with alarm or lack of trust. In our relationships, trust allows our deers/dears to stay and feel comfortable, while wariness creates confusion and bewilderment, like "a deer in the headlights." Sometimes we don't stop to think how our behavior will affect others (people or animals). We often do and say things without considering what reaction the deer/dear may have to it.

PERSONAL COMMENT
This poem is the telling of an actual event as it happened. After writing a short piece about someone from my past who had come to my mind, I took a break and walked outside my back door, into the cool evening air. I heard a frightened deer running away from the house and into the woods. I then heard the squeal of a car's brakes down by the road. I never learned whether that deer was hit. Later that evening, I showed my wife the short piece that I had written earlier, thinking she may find it art-worthy. She did not; on the contrary, her reaction was one of hurt, and she went upstairs to lay down. I thought of this coincidental parallel between the deer who may lay hurting outside by the road, and my wife who lay hurting upstairs. In response to that awareness, I wrote Parts 1 and 2 of this poem at the same sitting. The story—already lived—required only the matter of telling it in poetic format.

COMMON CENTS..Page 29

STRUCTURE
This poem is another one of those "sing-song" pieces, with four 4-line verses and a very elementary AABB rhyme scheme (á la "'Twas the Night Before Christmas"). The poem's fairly consistent iambic tetrameter meter is broken up only by the solo line, "No!" before the last verse, where the message pivots toward a more hopeful ending. On the surface, this piece is a simple story about a penny: Its structure and mottos; its "life journey"; and the ease with which it might be tossed aside due to the impact of its age on its worn surface. But it "doubles with age" and is worth even more, having been cherished throughout the years. The penny is an analogy for one's life partner.

IMAGERY
Clear visual images emerge from the simple description of the Penny in **Verse 1**: (see…both sides; head and tail) including the mottos therein. **Verse 2** presents a visual and olfactory image (fresh from the mint), and then it proceeds to personify the penny (it glints for spite; try as it might…stay upright; it stumbles…fumbles), followed by a double rhyme (rally of years, valley of tears.) **Verse 3** offers an aging feeling, along with a visual image (date wears old; luster fades). The call to "ha'penny" (which was a British half-pence) suggests that this penny is only worth half as much now than it was when it was new and shining, so "trade" it in, or toss into the wishing well (watch it sink). The "No!" creates a loud auditory image, and is followed in **Verse 4** by a more rational view of the now-cherished penny, suggesting that if not "tossed [nor] sold," it will be worth more than its "weight in gold."

THEMES
On the surface, the penny gains value with age and is therefore cherished more. Read with the analogy of one's life partner in mind, the poem is elevated to that of a philosophical treatise. On one's wedding day (or time of creation, if we go there with it) the "penny" is new, fresh, glinting. But then the "years" and the "tears" lead to "stumbles" and "fumbles" that cause it (him/her) to "fade." So why not just throw it away and get a new "penny?" Because "when we are gray," it (the relationship, the commitment; the person) will "outweigh its (his/her) weight in gold."

PERSONAL COMMENT
I am not sure when I wrote this piece (many years ago), but I suppose I knew then, as I know even more so now, that our "penny" is one that we can love and value forever. We do see both sides of it (him/her), and so we hold on tightly as we gray (must not be tossed; dare not be sold.) And doing so does makes sense (Common Cents).

Tom Blaisse

THE MIRACLES OF LIFE .... Page 33

STRUCTURE
This poem is another "standalone" piece in that it could be a nice greeting card. The simple yet eloquent five verses (of four lines each) capture the message with a consistent iambic trimeter meter and an airy ABCB rhyme scheme. As with a couple other poems in this book, each verse's Line 1 is the poem's title; each Line 2 completes the statement; and each verse's Lines 3 and 4 further explain its reasoning.

IMAGERY
Miracles can be interpreted as the reader may see fit. The images suggest options for interpretation.
- **Verse 1** suggests missing miracles due to our fast-paced life: occur...day; don't notice; rush along.
- **Verse 2** continues the theme, using angels as the metaphor: appear; drop in...angels; learn.
- **Verse 3:** child's toy; forgotten; lost joy.
- **Verse 4:** show up; answers; projected.
- **Verse 5:** climb...hill; power; shine...God's will.

THEMES
The consistent message in this poem is that miracles can be obvious, even ubiquitous. If we will just take time to *notice them*, we can learn from them. They are gifts from God, that just appear like "angels" or a "forgotten toy." "The answers...they give us" "help us climb each hill." We tend to forget about them, but if we stop and observe these simple miracles—and be grateful for them—we can be more in tune with God's plan for our lives.

PERSONAL COMMENT
In this poem, I use the word "miracles" in its simplest form; not as a major supernatural event, but as a subtle message from the Universe that we need to hear so that we can stay fresh and alive. The piece is personal because I strive to stay in tune with these little miracles; e.g., love that is conveyed through words or deeds; gratitude expressed; a lesson to be learned; an answer that has been sought. Without these "miracles," life might otherwise be flat and uninteresting.

LITTLE KIDS .... Page 34

STRUCTURE
With eight four-line verses spreading across two pages, this poem presents a traditional ABAB rhyme scheme. Lines 1 and 3 of each verse are in iambic tetrameter, and Lines 2 and 4 are in iambic trimeter. Due to the content of the piece, the childlike rhyme and cadence allow for a "sing-song" style in the reading of it. Verses 1–7 pose various similes, with a summary verse at the end providing a thematic conclusion.

IMAGERY
Each verse presents its own visual image in the opening line. Little kids are like the/a Sun, Moon, Rain, Star, Snow, Tree, Earth. Line 2 of each verse further defines the simile: shine, silver, refreshing, sparkles, falling, grow, resource. Then Lines 3 and 4 of each verse complete the verse, with thoughts about how little kids interact with our world, using vivid visual, auditory, and kinesthetic images: love to laugh…teach…play; hum…tune; feel…right; living…sane; loyal; glimmer…car; buffed with love; blankets; lullaby; see…fun…small; weight in gold; grow up. The final verse brings the reader back to the original image of little kids "sharing love."

THEMES
The key themes are obvious in the similes set up in the beginning of each verse: "Little kids are like…." The comparison is then followed up in each verse by further description of what kids are like, what they do, and why they are so valued. These comparisons and descriptions can be taken at face value with no underlying meaning. Each of the similes serves a purpose in our world, as do little kids, bringing us "love throughout the land."

PERSONAL COMMENT
I recall writing this poem after serving as Class Parent one morning at my daughter's kindergarten class (many years ago). Being the father of two older boys and (back then) a 5-year-old girl, I was no stranger to the activities and antics of little kids. However, that morning was very focused for me because my role was really just to observe, and assist if needed. While observing, I recognized the various roles that children play in their lives and how their behavior impacts our own lives. The metaphors seemed apparent to me as I watched them play and interact with each other and with their teacher.

A DIRECTOR'S NOTE .... Page 36

STRUCTURE
This poem is a bit different in style and format, with three seven-line verses. In each verse, Lines 1, 5, 6, and 7 are written in iambic tetrameter; Line 2 is iambic trimeter; and Lines 3 and 4 are iambic dimeter. There is no rhyme scheme here except for the couplet at the end. The poem progresses in its thought as the "play" is cast, rehearsed, and opens to "rave reviews." The "play" is an analogy for life and/or one's choice of a life partner. The rhyming couplet at the end purposely paraphrases a line from Shakespeare's *Hamlet*.

IMAGERY
On its literal level, the "Director" establishes visual, auditory, and kinesthetic images as the theatrical process unfolds.
- **Visual:** stage is set; the script; cast is set; every practice; play the play; must direct, be not directed; art will come; conscience of the king; the play's the thing.
- **Auditory:** says lines; gets called back; mute; not dumb; phrase the lines; critics rave; be still and listen.
- **Kinesthetic:** feels the part; reads with passion; choose...play the lead; fracture heals; move the scene; trust the script; pace the rhythm; if passion is there...; catch the conscience.

Reading the poem again with the proposed analogy in mind, that the "play" is one's life including one's choice of a life partner, note how the same images change in meaning.

THEMES
"All the world's a stage, And all the men and women merely players" (Shakespeare). Because our (life) drama unfolds as we direct it, "casting" is of utmost importance. Those key relationships that we choose to have in our life, especially the one who will be our life partner, will make or break the "play." As we move from adolescence to adulthood, there may be several possible casting choices and perhaps multiple "call backs." Ultimately, we cast in the lead role that special "one" who "best says lines" and "feels the part" with "passion." This major life decision helps the rest of our play fall into place. We should not second-guess that choice, but each day rehearse our play with art and craft, following—and trusting in—the (God's) script. If life is a rehearsal, then perhaps death is its "opening night," which will lead to the "critic's rave," provided we listen to and follow the "conscience of (our) King."

PERSONAL COMMENT
This is one of my favorite poems in the book because, having a strong Theatre background myself, I often relate life to the masks of Comedy and Tragedy. How we choose our cast and how well we direct our play is usually determined by our interpretation of, and attitude toward, life (the script.) For me, my casting choice has made all the difference in the world. My life would not have played out so well without my wonderful leading lady.

THE CHESS GAME .... Page 37

STRUCTURE
This poem contains four equally structured verses of six lines each. Lines 1, 5, and 6 of each verse are written in iambic tetrameter. Each verse's Line 3 has four beats; the first-half is iambic; the second-half is trochaic in its meter. Lines 2 and 4 are iambic dimeter. Additionally, Line 1 of each verse introduces the metaphor of the verse, followed by "'Tis a...." with a further explanation. Each line parallels its equivalent line in the other verses with the same word usage, sentence structure, and syntax, including a slight alliteration in Line 3 of each verse.

IMAGERY
The key image is, of course, that of a chess game. The "Move" refers to the chess player making his/her move on the board (of life), with each verse then setting up a metaphor with various visual, auditory, and kinesthetic images:

- **Visual:** stroke; simple spark; briefly lighted; playing space; victor's win; parlay (strategy); rightly armed; mounts in grandeur; finished scene; brush's stroke; single swipe; finely hued; vision clears; placed keenly.
- **Auditory:** calls (in silence); onetime echoed; versed (in step); lonely sounded; tuned for balance; total song; single note; first desired; sings in accord (as in a chord).
- **Kinesthetic:** (final) touch; fairly weighed; tension swells; inching itch; power climbs; marks in stillness; spirit sours.

THEMES
Chess, with its required strategies and patience, is frequently equated to "the game of life." We may often feel an intuitive desire to make our move ("a stroke of thought; a single spark..."). Yet we put that option on hold, to evaluate our other choices, often coming back to the original thought marked by our intuition (the "checking choice, first desired.) In **Verse 1**, that first consideration, though "fairly weighed and thus aligned with (the) playing space," keeps calling us back, especially under stress. **Verse 2** suggests that a single "move," if not "the victor's win" (using a military analogy) is the gamble (the "parlay") one might take because the idea seems so "versed in marching step." **Verse 3** compares the "move" to an artist, painting one stroke at time. **Verse 4** switches the metaphor to a single note in a song, which when "placed keenly in the measure," can lead to great "accord" (Check Mate).

PERSONAL COMMENT
Although somewhat convoluted in its imagery (and maybe because of it), this poem is one of my favorites. It does what ponderous poetry should do: Make the reader read it over again so as to figure out what it's really about. I rarely play chess, but I am familiar with the game. I often see in my own life "moves" that contribute to the win, and those that don't. Often my coming back to my first intuitive reaction after consideration of all other options really makes the difference. (See the poem "A Director's Note.")

Tom Blaisse

OR WHAT'S A HEAVEN FOR? .... Page 38

STRUCTURE
This poem is a sort of short lecture or motivational speech, with eight five-line verses. Lines 1, 3, 4, and 5 of each verse are in iambic tetrameter, with each Line 2 in iambic trimeter. Beginning with Robert Browning's famous verse, the poem expands into motivational content and goal-directed principles. It is written in the first-person plural, to include all in its messaging and universality, repeating "our," "we," and "us" often throughout the piece. Lines 2 and 4 of each verse are indented, to give it shape and style. There are also a few word plays and alliteration: often loftier; can come close; higher depths (oxymoron); mile…smile; year…tear; reveals…conceals…congeals; some…say…sights…seem silly; cause to pause; haunting….halt; love…live…light…learn.

IMAGERY
Visual: The Browning quote sets up the first visual images—reach, grasp, heaven—followed by others: vision; speed of light; springs us to action; dreams alive; sparked us; higher depths; exceed our grasp; smile; tear; sights…silly; Light of God; stay…Righteous Path; rewards…labor; room at the inn; forge a path; heaven.
Kinesthetic: anticipation; propel us; beliefs spring us; action…dreams alive; sparked us to commit; strive again; earthly climb; growth; fuel desire; persist; succeed; spur…cause to pause; drive us; pitfalls…stumbles; haunting…halt; weary bones…rest; love…harmony; we'll seek.

THEMES
Success is in the striving and the climbing—consistent with the theme of this book's title poem. Although goals need to be "lofty," they must also be realistic so that our belief that we can accomplish them becomes the initial motivating force (fuels desire), which is then sustained by persistence. Hope serves as the sustenance that allows us to continue on our journey, knowing that failure comes only from lack of striving and/or learning. Verses 6 and 7 pose the obstacles that may be placed in our way. The last verse concludes with the reminder that it is all worth it.

PERSONAL COMMENT
I rewrote this poem several times, to clarify its message and bring structure to it. The key concepts in the piece are consistent with the themes that I work with in my role as a Speaker, Organizational Consultant, and Seminar Leader. I like the way it unfolds in its thought, using the psychology of human motivation for its delivery pathway (Needs, Beliefs, Actions, Results). And from a more esoteric standpoint, I acknowledge that hope keeps us learning, which "fuels (the) desire" for us to keep striving. In the end, it is Persistence that will lead us to our success. As long as we resist the temptations of others, there will be "room at the inn."

We Are Climbers, All

THE CANDLE FLAME ....Page 40

STRUCTURE
With a short topic opener revealing the key metaphor, followed by four verses of seven equal lines of iambic tetrameter (with no rhyme scheme), each line cascades down the verse, as wax might drip down a candle. The first line of each verse sets up the image, one God-Person each from the Trinity, with a summary verse bringing the "Flame" together. The rest of the lines in each verse further define the stated image, with each Line 3 echoing a repetitive "'Tis the...." The ample alliteration in the poem adds to the color of the lines: Father figure; steady stream; hollow heat; softly sees; divining dawn; forward flow; shadow shining; circling Spirit; separate slices; burning brightly.

IMAGERY
Due to the imagery of this poem, interpretation may be a slightly daunting challenge. Although the introductory line sets up the key metaphor and Verses 1–3 are clear in their respective subject matter, the definitions and metaphors might need clarification.
- **Verse 1:** God, the Father—the "Earthy Root"—is the "wick" that holds the power for the candle to burn (the wax as fuel). It merges with the actual base of the flame itself (the hollow heat,) which is the Creator, who "brings life to light."
- **Verse 2:** God, the Son—the "Fire Tunnel"—is the inner strand of the candle flame, the "Saving Grace," that "softly sees with floral lids" (all knowing, yet ever forgiving). The "see-through glaze" suggests an illustrious transparency (a sacred heart) thus "connecting lives."
- **Verse 3:** God, the Holy Spirit—the Paraclete—is the "Rising Tip" (of the flame), the Comforter, the "shadow shining, alone in Virtue." It "circles...dances and prances" creating self-awareness for those who are willing to be open and receptive ("breathes in Art").
- **Verse 4:** God, the Flame—"wholly merged" from "separate slices of single Beauty" (three persons in One God)...never changing. What "might be hidden" (by the world) always "becomes aglow." Yet "if it be smothered, there is another" candle flame "burning brightly."

THEMES
The candle flame is the perfect metaphor for the Trinity as described above. The three Persons in one God serve as a single "Flame" linked together (base, tunnel, and tip), to forever light the world. "You are the light of the world" (Matthew 5:14). We cannot "hide our (His) light under a bushel," but rather we should exalt in the "endless, lilting pure illumined...power (that exists) from God, The Trinity, "shattering the darkness" by "standing straight."

PERSONAL COMMENT
I recall the moment of staring into a candle flame many years ago (while in a somewhat "relaxed" state of mind), dismantling the three parts of that flame, and equating them to the three persons of the Trinity. At that time, I wrote the original words in a stream of consciousness, only now going back to edit and format the piece for this book.

Tom Blaisse

THE PRODUCTIVITY PYRAMID............................ Page 41

STRUCTURE
Seven four-line verses with an ABAB rhyme scheme make this poem structured and stylized. The content is derived from the FranklinCovey Co. *Time Management* workshop, and the verses build upon the pyramid model that is used in that program. In each verse, Lines 1 and 3 are in iambic tetrameter; Lines 2 and 4 are iambic trimeter. Note that the piece is written in the first-person singular, allowing the reader to affirm his/her commitment to laying in each block of the model.

IMAGERY
The picture of the pyramid next to the poem represents the "building blocks" for one's increased personal productivity. The opening verse poses the awareness question: "Where has the time gone?" The rest of the verses offer varied complementary images:
    Visual: firmly fit; purpose...manifest; bridge the values gap; pay life's tolls; measureable map; see results; distractions I'll resist.
    Auditory: values calling; mission's call.
    Kinesthetic: deepening thirst; strength to harbor wit; crave to build; challenge of change; break down the goals; working SMART; success...persist; balance...fun; Inner Peace.

THEMES
The key (time management) message in this poem is that by "controlling the events of our lives, we can increase our personal productivity and self-esteem." It all begins with identifying and committing to our "Governing Values," and then setting "Long-Range Goals" that are Specific, Measurable, Action-oriented, Realistic, and Time-framed (SMART), to reflect those Values. We then need to break those goals down into "Intermediate Goals," and write the related work actions on our "Daily Task" list. Resisting "Time Robbers" (matters that may be urgent but not important long-term) and including some recreational activities for balance keeps us focused on success and increases our work/life time productivity and effectiveness, which leads to "Inner Peace."

PERSONAL COMMENT
I worked for FranklinCovey Co. (formerly Franklin Quest) as a Seminar Leader for more than 10 years (1989-2000), and conducted close to 1,800 "Time Quest" workshops for more than 50,000 participants. The seminar was a "life-changing" experience that empowered people to take control of their time and their lives by building their "Productivity Pyramid" and using the Franklin Day Planner as their implementation tool and record-keeping book. I was inspired to write this poem by the work I was doing during those years and the pyramid graphic that served as the program model.

We Are Climbers, All

JUST DO IT!...Page 42

STRUCTURE
In Verses 1—3, Line 1 presents the reader with a repeating self-examination question about his/her procrastination. Each Line 1 includes a play on words: busy...busi-ness; fearful...fearless; thoughtful....thoughtless. Those lines are written in Trochee tetrameter (stressed then unstressed) as opposed to the usual iambic meter used for most of the other poems in this book. Lines 2–5 of each verse are written in Trochee trimeter, and are indented, to offset each Verse's Line 1. Those four lines in each verse begin with an *'ing* word, to define ways that one may be putting things off or trying to escape from getting things done. The last verse, also written in Trochee tetrameter, sets up the motivational directive using strong action verbs: stop; change; set; ignore; take the time...contemplate; make the plan...activate. The "button up" line at the end of the piece suggests the payoff (Illusive Inner Peace.).

IMAGERY
The *'ing* words not only define ways that we might procrastinate, they also set up many kinesthetic images. (Please refer back to the poem for these.) The visual images at the end of each line complete the thought with a vivid picture for the reader. (Again, please refer back to the poem.) The final verse kicks into high gear, with the action verbs ending with exclamation points, to underscore the desired feeling coming from the urgency. The last line provides a resting image of Inner Peace.

THEMES
Bringing back the *Time Management* themes from "The Productivity Pyramid," this poem focuses on ways that one might shirk responsibility or commitment to a previously identified task or goal. We often fall "below the line" (*The Oz Principle*), avoiding or denying what "it" is that needs to get done, or that there's a problem that must be solved. The old Nike commercial slogan reminds us to stop putting things off and "Just do it!"

PERSONAL COMMENT
Harkening back again to my previous tenure with FranklinCovey Co., the "time robbers" tend to get in the way of our ability to focus on what really matters most. We often seem to be too "busy" to be "productive." Additionally, our fears and thoughtlessness often distort our focus and clarity. Example: I've been putting off editing and publishing this book of poems for years, until I decided to just do it!

RENEWAL .... Page 43

STRUCTURE
With seven verses of four lines each, written in iambic tetrameter, this poem reveals a personal story, beginning and ending with the same thought, as the verses unfold from past to present to future. Verse 1 sets up what had happened, with Verse 2 jumping to the present. Verses 3 and 4 then reflect on how it can happen, while Verse 5 brings the reader back to the present. Verse 6 stays in the present except for the first line, which quickly reflects back to the past. Verse 7 then wraps up the story and looks into the future. Examples of alliteration and other word plays include: found...fuel...fondle; burns brightly, lightly; life...lost...longing...lain. Although most of the poem does not rhyme, Verse 4 contains an unexpected AAAA rhyme scheme, with verse 7 holding an AABB rhyme.

IMAGERY
Various types of images add flavor to the story this poem tells:
  Visual: walled; hollow tube; found the fuel; fire stirred...burns brightly;
    stage is dark; upon...perch; bleaker set; pried me open; form and substance;
    finding Truth; life...lost...longing...lain; smiles...newly lit.
  Auditory: express I now; hear the meaning; share each moment; no longer feud.
  Kinesthetic: taste of innocence; dullness; spark of passion; fondle warmth;
    air to breathe; cheerful; ponder answers; sullen; doubt and fear...inhibit life;
    balance...strive; thrive; joy; shock of folly; been renewed.

THEMES
As the title implies, renewal is the key message throughout the poem. Without knowing it, we can easily shut down "into a hollow tube of dullness" until some event in our lives wakes us up (spark of passion; new career; family life). Thinking is good unless it is negative ("sullen on a bleaker set"), so our "thought and feelings [need to be in] balance" in order to find the "Truth," which can "shock" us from our "folly" and help us express a "reborn spirit." We need to accept ourselves for who we are ("no longer feud") so we can each day feel renewed.

PERSONAL COMMENT
This poem reveals the feeling I developed over a long period of time, after I had "settled down" into family life; felt secure in my career (with FranklinCovey Co., at that time); and began to finally enjoy life on life's terms. When I wrote this poem (many years ago), I did not fully realize the relevance of the last verse. These days, I understand how important it is to rekindle the renewal process one day at a time.

WE ARE CLIMBERS, ALL ....Page 44

STRUCTURE
As a stream of consciousness piece, this poem originally had no verses or indentation. To make it more readable, it now consists of six (admittedly uneven) verses, with each verse cascading down from left to right, mirroring a mountain ledge. With no rhyme scheme or consistent rhythm, most of the lines follow a loose 3–5 beat cadence. Verse 1 sets up the "problem," suggesting that our "dream" is to "touch the sky," with the "mountain" being both the obstacle and the vehicle. Verse 2 confirms the "humanity" of the challenge, with the shorter Verse 3 setting up the pivotal point for the reader. Verse 4 then moves toward the climax of this short story, with Verse 5 offering the emotion behind it, and Verse 6 the resolution.

IMAGERY
The mountain itself is the main visual image, rising up to frustrate our dreams. **Verse 1** presents keen visual and kinesthetic images as unrealistic options: no lift; no plane to ride; nor birds who soar and perch; nor spirit...gravity. **Verse 2** offers strong, almost painful, images: humanity hurts; scrapes...bruises; slip and grab; (loss of) courage; pebbles tumble...smarts; fear the fall; chance the move. **Verse 3** encourages the reader to "hold steady" (onto the proverbial rope) as the (pebbles tumble), yet the (reign of terror) is short-lived; swing the height; aching joy...joyous ache. **Verse 4** empowers the reader: kiss the ledge; flatland reached; the goal...injects...strength; leap on top; dance in air. **Verse 5**: taming the surge; floods the soul; passion... deeper; flower...sweeter; star...brighter. **Verse 6**: look up...look down; scratches heal...gladness swells; dream becomes alive.

THEMES
Life itself is the challenge if we desire to achieve our earthly goals or strive for heaven. "[Our] reach should exceed [our] grasp, or what's a heaven for?" (Robert Browning). As we face the vicissitudes of daily life, we must "hold steady" as the "pebbles tumble," remembering that the "reign of terror comes up short." (Another way of saying "This too shall pass.") We keep climbing until we get so close that *the belief in our success* is in itself the final motivator as well as its own reward.

PERSONAL COMMENT
I chose this poem for the title of the book because it embraces the key themes of "Learning, Loving, and Living." I wrote this piece the day after my graduation from graduate school. I had quit halfway through the program, and then 18 months later, I went back to finish earning my degree. I was still teaching high school at the time, and the Seniors were taking one of their final exams. As they did their work (striving to achieve their own goal), I sat at my desk in Room 244, pouring out my feelings about the journey that I had once embraced; then abandoned; and later rekindled. There was indeed for me "no taming the surge that flood(ed) the soul with heaven." This poem represents my life's key message, mission, and legacy.

ABOUT THE AUTHOR
Tom Blaisse

Tom Blaisse holds a B.A. in Theatre and Speech from DeSales University in Allentown, PA, and an M.A. in Counseling Psychology from Rider University in Trenton, NJ.

During the almost 11 years Tom served as a Senior Consultant with FranklinCovey Co. (formerly Franklin Quest), he presented *Time Management* and *Stress Management* seminars to thousands of people each year.

Tom is currently President of TFB Consulting (TomBlaisse.com), a Human Resources Training & Development company in Harrisburg, PA. As a Keynote Speaker and Seminar Leader on a variety of performance effectiveness topics, Tom helps corporate clients establish and develop dynamic learning organizations. He is also a certified Executive Facilitator for several regional and national management consulting firms. Tom is a member of the American Society for Training and Development (ASTD), and the National Speakers' Association (NSA).

Avocationally, Tom is an actor, director, singer, songwriter, poet, and playwright. He has co-authored five musical plays for children, and has also written the music and lyrics for more than a dozen contemporary Christian songs, under the title *Manifest the Glory of God*.

Tom lives in Harrisburg, PA, with his wife Roberta ("Cookie"). Their almost-empty nest holds many fond memories of raising their three children, Matthew, Michael, and Beth, who, as young adults, are now "climbing their own mountains."

We Are Climbers, All

NOTES

Tom Blaisse

NOTES

Made in the USA
Columbia, SC
12 July 2018